12/01

DY1

Tornadoes

By Christy Steele

Steadwell Books

Raintree Steck-Vaughn Publishers
A Harcourt Company

Austin · New York
www.steck-vaughn.com

Nature
on the
Rampage

Published by Raintree Steck-Vaughn Publishers,
an imprint of Steck-Vaughn Company.

Library of Congress Cataloging-in-Publication Data
Steele, Christy.
     Tornadoes/by Christy Steele.
          p.cm.--(Nature on the rampage)
     Includes index.
     Summary: Introduces the causes and environmental effects of
tornadoes.
     ISBN 0-7398-1794-9
     1. Tornadoes--Juvenile literature. [1. Tornadoes.] I. Title. II.
Series.
QC955.2 .S74 2000
551.55'3--dc21

                                                            99-058670

Printed in the United States of America
10 9 8 7 6 5 4 3 2 1 LB 02 01 00

Produced by Compass Books

Photo Acknowledgments
Digital Stock, cover, title page, 4, 11, 12, 17, 20, 24,
     26, 29

Content Consultant
Harold Brooks, Ph.D.
National Severe Storms Laboratory
Norman, Oklahoma

CONTENTS

ABOUT TORNADOES

A tornado is made of fast winds that spin. It is the strongest windstorm on Earth. Its spinning winds can blow at speeds of more than 300 miles (483 km) an hour. A tornado can be a few feet wide or more than 1 mile (1.6 km) wide.

Tornadoes can strike any time of the year. Most tornadoes happen in the months from March to August. These spring and summer months make up tornado season. About 1,000 tornadoes hit the United States during tornado season.

 This tornado in Kansas is just a few feet wide.

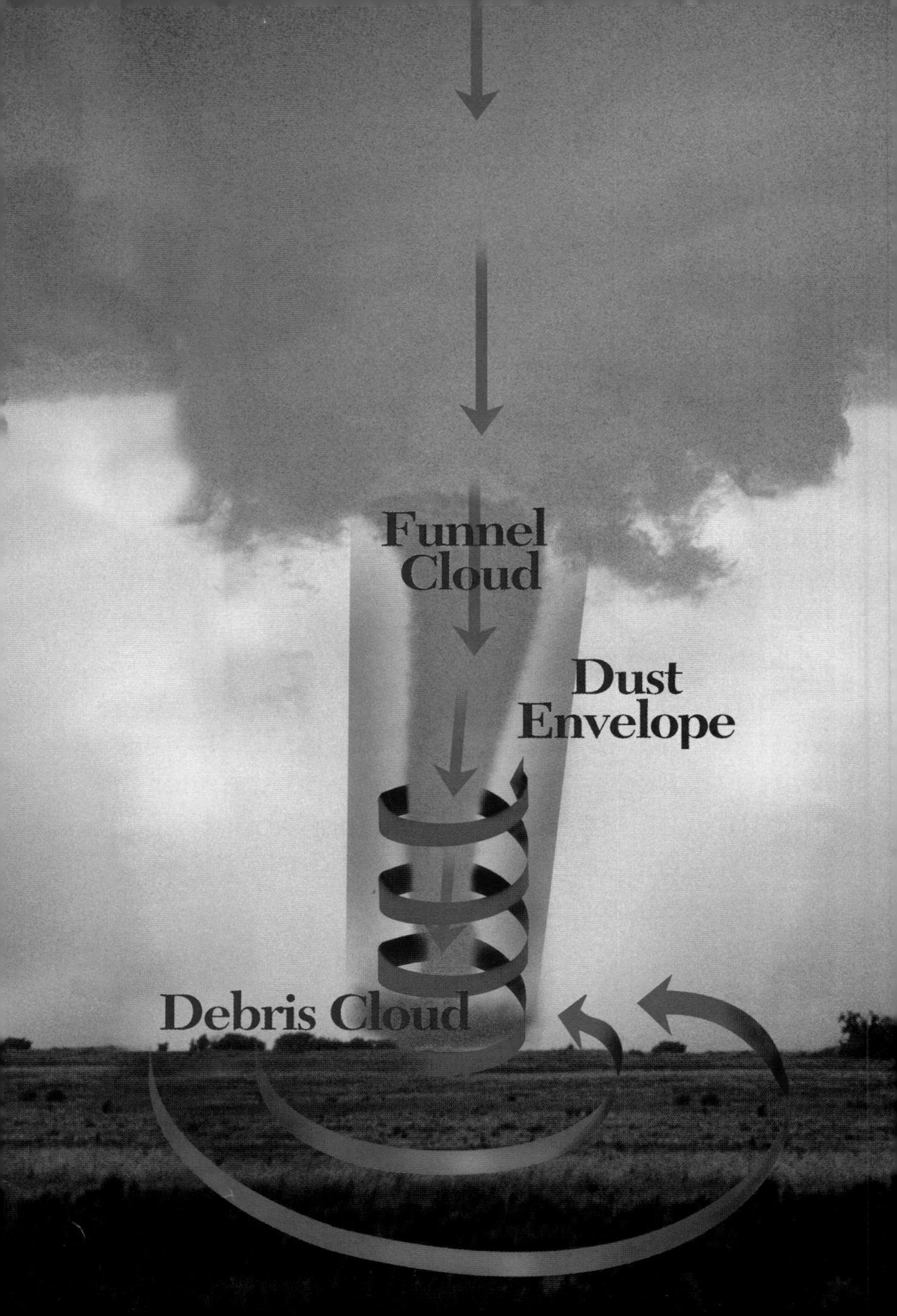
Funnel
Cloud
Dust
Envelope
Debris Cloud

A Tornado Begins

Most tornadoes start in supercell thunderstorms. Supercells have clouds more than 6 miles (9.6 km) high. Heavy rain and hail can fall from these clouds. Hail is made up of small chunks of ice that fall from the sky.

Supercells start when cold, dry air mixes with warm, moist air. Moist air has much water in it. The water in the warm air cools as it rises. It falls back to Earth as rain.

Tornadoes begin when warm air rises quickly and begins to spin. This can make a funnel cloud. A funnel cloud looks like a funnel. A funnel is a long cone with an open end at its bottom. A funnel cloud becomes a tornado if it reaches the ground. The winds in a tornado pick up dust, dirt, and debris from the ground. Debris can be things like parts of trees, sand, and cars.

Many tornadoes can grow from one supercell. Tornadoes often end when the supercell ends. A tornado can last from a few seconds to a few hours. Most tornadoes last from two to three minutes.

 This diagram shows the parts of a tornado.

Where Tornadoes Happen

Tornadoes can happen anywhere in the world. India, Bangladesh, and Australia have many tornadoes. In 1989, a tornado in Bangladesh killed about 1,300 people.

Most tornadoes happen in the Great Plains of North America. People often call part of the Great Plains Tornado Alley because of the many tornadoes that happen there. States in Tornado Alley are Nebraska, Kansas, Oklahoma, and Texas.

How Tornadoes Move

Each tornado moves differently. Some tornadoes take straight paths. Some zigzag. Other tornadoes move in small circles on the ground. One tornado can travel in different kinds of paths.

Tornadoes can grow bigger or smaller as they travel. In some places, a damage path may be 1 mile (1.6 km) wide. In other places, it may be 2 miles (3 km) wide.

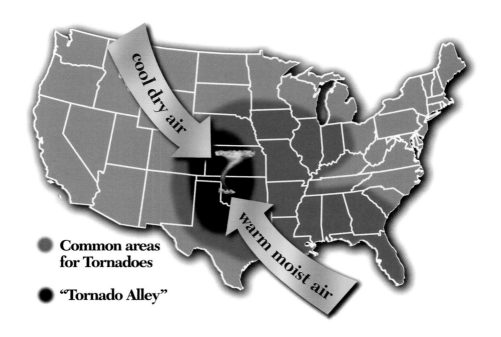

- Common areas for Tornadoes
- "Tornado Alley"

cool dry air

warm moist air

Warm, moist air and cold, dry air meet in Tornado Alley. The mixing air causes many tornadoes.

Meteorologists are scientists who study weather. They measure the size and wind speed of a tornado by the path of damage it leaves. Damage is harm or injury that causes loss or makes something less valuable.

Warning Signs of a Tornado

Tornadoes often start quickly. Watching the weather for signs of a tornado can give people time to reach a safe place.

- Funnel clouds may turn into tornadoes.
- The sky may appear slightly green or green-black before a tornado.
- The air may become still right before a tornado.
- A strong thunderstorm that makes hail also may start tornadoes.
- Noise may mean a tornado is near. A tornado's winds sound like a train or airplane.

A Tornado's Color

A tornado's color depends on the debris it carries. Tornadoes that carry mostly dust and dirt are dark gray. Tornadoes carrying the colored dirt of the Southwest look red-orange. Tornadoes above water are called waterspouts. Waterspouts pull up water and appear blue.

A tornado's color also depends on the light. Tornadoes seem white if the sun is shining on them. Tornadoes seem gray if they are in the shadow of the sun.

This tornado has sucked up dirt from the farm field it ripped apart.

KILLER TORNADOES

Scientists in the early 1900s studied the weather to find out how tornadoes started. But they did not have all the right tools they needed to understand weather.

Without helpful tools, scientists were not able to warn people about tornadoes. To warn is to tell someone about danger. Tornadoes were more deadly in the past because people had no warnings.

 About 42 people in North America die in tornadoes each year.

Fujita-Pearson Tornado Scale

Scientists use the Fujita-Pearson Tornado Scale to rate how powerful tornadoes are. Scientists study the damage a tornado causes. They then give the tornado a number from F0 to F5. Powerful tornadoes receive higher numbers than weak tornadoes.

Most tornadoes are F0 or F1. These weak tornadoes do little damage. They may blow branches off trees. Only about one in 100 tornadoes are F5. These killer tornadoes can blow down buildings and trees.

Some Killer Tornadoes

The most tornadoes to strike the United States in one day happened from April 3 to 4, 1974. About 148 tornadoes touched down. The tornadoes blew down every building in several towns. They smashed homes, schools, and police stations. The tornadoes caused $600 million in damage. They killed 315 people.

In April 1998, one huge supercell started a line of strong F3 and F4 tornadoes. The tornadoes ripped through Mississippi, Alabama, and Georgia. They blew down hundreds of buildings. More than 36 people died.

Fujita-Pearson Tornado Scale

F-5

Wind Speed: 261 to 318 miles (420 to 512 km) an hour
Damage: Winds level everything in their path. The tornado lifts houses and smashes them against the ground. Winds send vehicles flying through the air.

F-4

Wind Speed: 207 to 260 miles (333 to 419 km) an hour
Damage: Winds blow down building walls. Tornado lifts vehicles and debris. Winds uproot trees and break their trunks in half.

F-3

Wind Speed: 158 to 206 miles (254 to 332 km) an hour
Damage: Winds tear off roofs. Tornado blows down trees and overturns cars.

F-2

Wind Speed: 113 to 157 miles (182 to 253 km) an hour
Damage: Winds damage houses and trees.

F-1

Wind Speed: 73 to 112 miles (117 to 181 km) an hour
Damage: Winds may damage roofs and signs.

F-0

Wind Speed: 40 to 72 miles (64 to 116 km) an hour
Damage: Winds break tree branches.

May 1999 Tornadoes

On May 3, 1999, several supercell storms blew into Oklahoma. Many strong tornadoes started in these storms. People saw at least 70 tornadoes in Oklahoma, Kansas, and Texas.

At least 26 tornadoes made damage paths through Oklahoma. Strong F4 tornadoes picked up cars and threw them into buildings. The tornadoes were the most costly in Oklahoma history. It cost more than $1 billion to fix the tornado damage.

Meteorologists gave people warnings about the May tornadoes. The warnings saved many lives. But the tornadoes still killed 40 people. More than 675 people were hurt.

The Oklahoma tornadoes started in a supercell thunderstorm like this one.

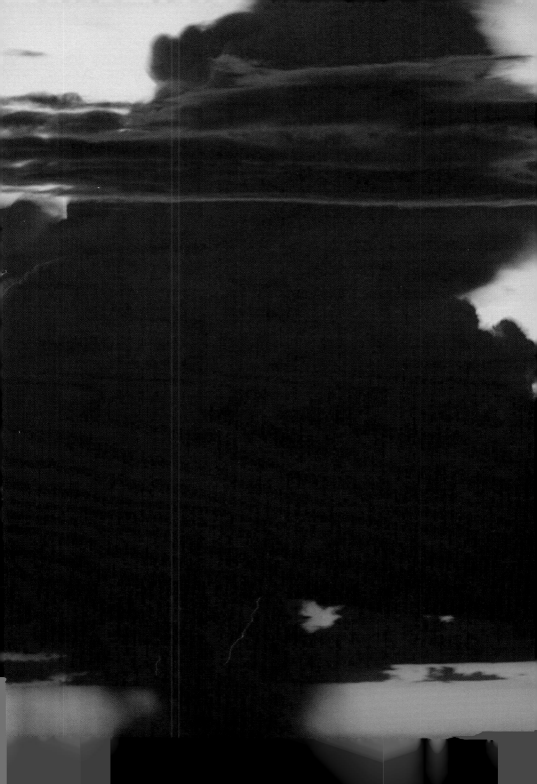

Weird Winds

A tornado's winds can do strange things. A tornado blew the walls of a building away. But it left standing the shelves that leaned against the walls. Nothing fell off of the shelves. A tornado lifted five train cars and carried them away. Another tornado pulled 16 students from their chairs. It put the students down 450 feet (137 m) away. The students lived. But the tornado smashed the school.

Tornadoes may carry animals into the air. One tornado in France lifted the water, fish, and frogs from a pond. The tornado dropped the fish and frogs miles away. People thought it was raining fish and frogs.

One tornado lifted a herd of cows and sent them flying. They landed miles away. Many of the cows lived. Another tornado blew the feathers off chickens. The chickens lived.

A tornado's winds can blow things so strongly that everyday objects become dangerous. One tornado blew a piece of plastic through a tree trunk. Tornado winds can make blades of grass and straw cut through wood. Pieces of wood can break through concrete. In one tornado, a playing card stuck into a wood wall.

Three Deadliest U.S. Tornadoes

• Tri-State Tornado

On March 18, 1925, a tornado touched down in Missouri. It was so low and wide that people could not see its funnel. It looked like a black cloud moving across the ground. The tornado went about 200 miles (322 km) through Missouri, Illinois, and Indiana.

The Tri-State Tornado was the worst tornado in history. It blew down every building in four towns. It killed about 700 people. Flying debris hurt more than 2,000 people.

• Natchez Tornado

On May 7, 1840, a tornado touched down near Natchez, Mississippi. The tornado sucked up the trees along the banks of the Mississippi River. It also lifted rafts and steamboats off the river. It smashed them back into the water. Many boats sank and people drowned. The tornado killed 317 people. More than 100 people were hurt. This was the second worst tornado in U.S. history.

• St. Louis Tornado of 1896

On May 27, 1896, a tornado touched down in eastern St. Louis, Missouri. The tornado was about 1 mile (1.6 km) wide. It smashed houses, factories, hospitals, and railroad yards. About 255 people died in the St. Louis Tornado. More than 1,000 people were hurt. The death count makes it the third worst tornado in U.S. history.

TORNADO SAFETY

Meteorologists today use special tools to find out when tornadoes and other storms will strike. Meteorologists warn people when tornadoes might happen.

Meteorologists give a tornado watch during bad weather that can cause a tornado. People should listen to radio and television news during tornado watches. They should stay close to a safe place in case a tornado starts.

 Some scientists now think that lightning can help them figure out where tornadoes will start.

Tornado Myths

Early people told stories called myths to explain weather. In myths, powerful beings like the ones mentioned below were in charge of the weather.

• **In North America**, some American Indians believed that the Great Spirit sent tornadoes to punish people who did bad things. Other American Indians believed tornadoes destroyed old things so new things could begin.

• **The Aztecs** believed the wind-god Ehecatl was in charge of the air. He looked like a dancing monkey. The Aztecs believed Ehecatl blew the Sun across the sky each day. They believed tornadoes and other windstorms came from Ehecatl blowing down on Earth.

• **In Asia,** Japanese people believed the wind-god Fujin controlled the air. They thought Fujin sent tornadoes and storms. People in India believed that Indra was a god who made the weather. Indra sent tornadoes to hurt bad people.

Warnings and Shelters

Meteorologists give a tornado warning if someone sees a tornado. Tornado sirens often sound during a tornado warning. People should treat tornado warnings seriously. They should go to a safe place right away.

Tornado shelters are safe places to go during tornado warnings. These shelters are below ground. A tornado blows over the shelters, and people inside stay safe. People can take cover in the lowest level of a building. A basement is best. People should find a room with no windows. Closets and bathrooms without windows are good places to take cover.

Never try to outrun a tornado. Do not try to watch or film a tornado. Never stay in cars during a tornado. Leave cars and find a building. Or find the nearest low part of dry ground such as a ditch. Then lie down in it.

Tornado Safety

People living in high-risk tornado areas should have a tornado safety kit. The kit should have a flashlight and weather radio that runs on batteries. A weather radio gives people weather information 24 hours a day. The kit also should have water, canned food, blankets, medical supplies, and extra batteries.

People should have tornado drills to practice what to do during a tornado. Everyone needs to know the safest places to go. Everyone should be able to reach safe places quickly. Someone should be in charge of bringing the tornado safety kit. People should practice getting down low. They should cover their heads with their arms and hands. This will help protect their bodies from flying debris.

 A tornado lifted and dropped these cars.

TORNADOES AND SCIENCE

Meteorologists still have questions about tornadoes. Scientists do not know what paths tornadoes will take. They do not know how big tornadoes will grow.

Meteorologists gather information about tornadoes to answer their questions. They study it to help them find out when and where tornadoes will begin. Scientists want to know how strong tornadoes will become.

This meteorologist is checking a weather map to look for storms.

Storm Chasers

Scientists need to see tornadoes to gather the best information. Some scientists do this by finding and chasing storms. A machine called Doppler radar helps scientists find tornadoes. It measures wind speeds and rainfall. Scientists watch Doppler radar to find supercells that may create tornadoes.

Specially trained volunteer tornado spotters also help scientists find tornadoes. Volunteers are not paid for their help. Tornado spotters tell scientists about any tornadoes they see.

Storm chasers drive close to storms once they find them. They take pictures and videos of the storms. They study winds and damage paths.

Future of Tornado Science

Scientists now think that tornadoes may start under clouds where much lightning flashes back and forth. People often cannot see lightning that flashes between clouds. They use a new machine called the Optical Transient Detector (OTD) to find lightning flashes that people cannot see. The OTD may help scientists find out when and where tornadoes will start.

▲ **This funnel cloud started in a supercell. It turned into a weak tornado.**

In the future, scientists will learn more about tornadoes. Scientists are making new machines that can be lifted by tornadoes. These machines will send information about the insides of tornadoes back to scientists.

Scientists hope that new information will help them give earlier tornado warnings. Better warnings will help save people's lives.

GLOSSARY

debris (di-BREE)—flying objects carried by tornadoes

Doppler radar (RAY-dahr)—a machine that measures wind speed and rainfall

funnel cloud (FUHN-uhl CLOWD)—a cloud shaped like a funnel; a funnel cloud looks like an upside-down cone with an open end at its bottom

hail (HALE)—small chunks of ice that fall from the sky

meteorologist (mee-tee-or-OL-oh-jist)—a scientist who studies weather

supercell (SOO-pur-cell)—a large, strong thunderstorm made up of huge clouds

volunteer (vahl-uhn-TIR)—someone who does a job without pay

waterspout (WAH-tur-spowt)—a tornado that forms over water

▼ Addresses and Internet Sites

National Severe Storms Laboratory
1313 Halley Circle
Norman, OK 73069

National Weather Service
1325 East West Highway
Silver Spring, MD 20910

FEMA for Kids: The Disaster Area
http://www.fema.gov/kids/dizarea.htm

National Severe Storms Laboratory
http://www.nssl.noaa.gov

National Skywarn
http://www.skywarn.org

The Tornado Project Online
http://www.tornadoproject.com

Twister!
http://whyfiles.news.wisc.edu/013tornado/index.
html

INDEX

Australia, 8
Aztecs, 22

Bangladesh, 8

debris, 7, 10, 19, 25
Doppler radar, 28

Fujin, 22
Fujita-Pearson
   Tornado Scale, 14, 15
funnel cloud, 7, 10, 19

hail, 7, 10

India, 8, 22

Mississippi River, 19

Natchez, Mississippi,
   19

safety kit, 25
St. Louis, Missouri, 19
sirens, 23
storm chasers, 28
supercell, 7, 14, 16, 28

Tornado Alley, 8
tornado drills, 25
tornado season, 5
tornado shelter, 23
tornado warning, 23
tornado watch, 21
Tri-State Tornado, 19

waterspout, 10
weather radio, 25